W9-BEZ-363

The Best
of EVERYTHING
HOCKEY
BOOK

by Shane Frederick

CAPSTONE PRESS
a capstone imprint

Sports Illustrated KIDS books are published by Capstone Press,
151 Good Counsel Drive, P.O. Box 669, Mankato, Minnesota 56002.
www.capstonepub.com

Books published by Capstone Press are manufactured with paper
containing at least 10 percent post-consumer waste.

Library of Congress Cataloging-in-Publication Data
Frederick, Shane.
  The best of everything hockey book / by Shane Frederick.
     p. cm.—(All-time best of sports. Sports Illustrated kids)
  Includes bibliographical references and index.
  ISBN 978-1-4296-5469-2 (library binding)
  ISBN 978-1-4296-6328-1 (paperback)
  1. Hockey—Miscellanea—Juvenile literature. 2. Hockey—Records—Juvenile literature.
  3. Hockey teams—Juvenile literature. 4. National Hockey League—Juvenile literature.
  I. Title. II. Series.
  GV847.25.F73 2011
  796.962—dc22   2010038476

Editorial Credits
Anthony Wacholtz editor; Ashlee Suker, designer;
Eric Gohl, media researcher; Eric Manske, production specialist

Photo Credits
123RF/Rocco Macri, 50
AP Images/The Canadian Press, 22; Paul Connors, 45 (t)
Getty Images Inc./Bruce Bennett Studios, 19, 23 (b), 24 (b), 25 (t), 44, 57 (t)
iStockphoto/Joseph Gareri, cover (background); spxChrome, cover (puck), 1
Library of Congress, 60 (t)
Newscom/KRT/Roy Gallop, 15 (b); Louis Deluca, 42 (b); MCT/Ralph Lauer, 43
Shutterstock/Fahrner, 57 (b); Marty Ellis, 36–37 (background), 45 (b); Nip, 8–9 (rink);
    Rob Marmion 10–11; Zeliksone Veronika, 38 (t)
Sports Illustrated/Bob Martin, 54 (b); Bob Rosato, 17, 25 (b), 31 (bl), 47 (b); Damian Strohmeyer, cover
    (tr & br), 14 (b), 47 (t); David E. Klutho, cover (tl, bl, bml, bm, bmr), 4–5, 6, 9 (t & br), 11 (t), 13, 14 (t),
    16, 24 (t), 26 (b), 27 (t & bmr), 28 (b), 29 (ml & mr), 30 (r), 31 (bmr), 32 (t), 33 (b, all), 36 (r), 37 (t & m),
    38 (b), 39 (t), 40 (all), 41 (all), 46 (b), 48 (t), 49, 51, 52 (t), 55 (all), 56 (all), 59 (all), 61; Heinz Kluetmeier,
    23 (t), 54 (t); Hy Peskin, 12, 27 (bl & br), 31 (t), 39 (b), 52 (b); John D. Hanlon, 28 (m), 35 (t), 53; John
    G. Zimmerman, 31 (br); John Iacono, 20 (t), 46 (t), 60 (b); Manny Millan, 29 (r), 36 (l); Richard Meek,
    26 (t); Robert Beck, 7, 28 (t), 32 (b), 33 (t), 34 (b), 42 (t), 58; Tony Triolo, 15 (t), 20–21 (b), 27 (bml), 29 (l),
    30 (l), 31 (bml), 34 (t), 35 (b), 37 (b); Walter Iooss Jr., 21 (t)
Wikimedia/Kendrick Erickson, 48 (b); spcbrass, 18

Printed in the United States of America in North Mankato, Minnesota.

092010   005933CGS11

TABLE OF CONTENTS

INTRODUCTION

"It's a great day for hockey!"

—Bob Johnson, hockey coach

Bob Johnson spent just six seasons as a coach in the National Hockey League, but he made an enormous impact in that short time. He took the Calgary Flames all the way to the Stanley Cup finals in 1986, and he lifted the Cup as a champion with the Pittsburgh Penguins in 1991. Before going to the NHL, Johnson coached the University of Wisconsin Badgers. There he won three national titles and received the nickname "Badger Bob."

Although the Penguins repeated as champions in 1992, Johnson was not there. He had to step down from his post because of brain cancer, and he died in 1991.

Johnson loved the game of hockey and tried to pass his enthusiasm on to his players, whether they were college kids or veteran professionals. His famous catchphrase, "It's a great day for hockey," is still celebrated both in Wisconsin and in Pittsburgh.

It's easy to see why enthusiasm surrounds hockey. The sport has speed and skill, hard hits, and intensity. Game-winning goals are celebrated with group hugs, and even the fiercest rivals line up and shake hands after a grueling playoff series. Each game opens the possibility for an amazing goal or a shocking check into the boards. Read on to learn about the best of the best on ice.

CHAPTER 1

THE GAME

LET'S PLAY HOCKEY

The play begins with a bone-crushing hit. The defenseman drives the opposing puck carrier into the boards, rattling the glass. He scoops up the puck as his victim falls to the ice. The defenseman passes it ahead to a forward flying through the neutral zone. The forward catches the puck and makes a fancy move to get around a defender. He fakes a shot during the breakaway to get the goalie moving. He follows the fake with a rocket shot that sends the puck over the goalie's shoulder and into the net. Goal!

A big hit, a beautiful pass, a crazy deke, and a goal. It's the perfect combination to send any crowd into a frenzy, whether it's at a city rink, a high school arena, or a 20,000-seat NHL stadium.

THE EVOLUTION OF HOCKEY

The game of hockey that we know today looked much different in the 1800s, when the sport was invented. Long before there were pro teams in southern California, Texas, and Florida—and even a few years before the game moved indoors—the rules were much different than they are now.

The object of hockey was the same: Score goals by shooting a small, flat puck into your opponent's net while trying to stop the opposing team from doing the same. But in the late 1800s, it was not the high-flying, hard-hitting, wide-open game we watch today. Back then players were not allowed to pass the puck forward. Lifting the puck off the ice while taking a shot on goal was illegal too.

But hockey is an ever-evolving game. The rules have been tweaked since the first player got slashed across the wrists. Eventually the game opened up, and players were allowed to pass the puck forward. First they could make such a pass only within one of the three zones. Later they were able to pass from the defensive zone to the neutral zone. The only offside rule remaining is when an attacking player crosses the blue line and into the offensive zone before the puck.

The rule about not lifting the puck when trying to shoot a goal was dismissed too. That's why goalies started wearing big pads, giant gloves, and facemasks.

THE RINK

The game of hockey was first played on the frozen lakes and ponds of Canada and the northern United States. When it comes to the NHL, the game is played in arenas and stadiums that hold as many as 20,000 fans. In most cases, the ice surface is 200 feet (61 meters) long and 85 feet (26 m) wide. Boards about 4 feet (1.2 m) high surround the ice to keep the puck in play. Safety glass is placed on top of the boards to protect the spectators from pucks. The rink is divided into three zones, two offensive/defensive zones and the neutral zone.

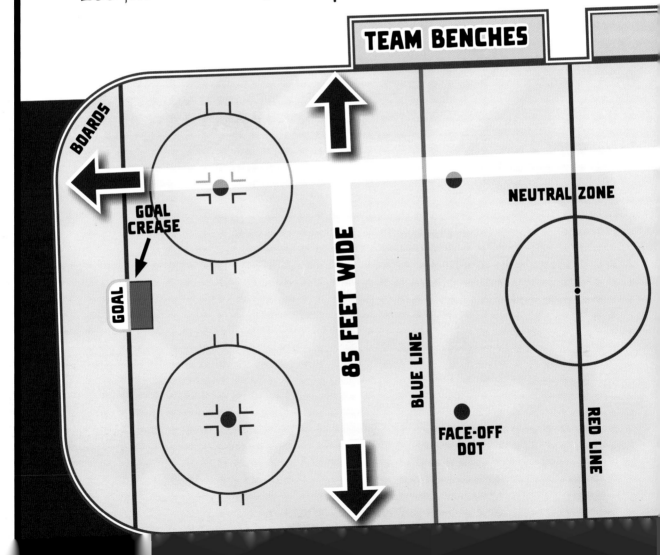

TEAM BENCHES

BOARDS

GOAL CREASE

GOAL

85 FEET WIDE

BLUE LINE

FACE-OFF DOT

NEUTRAL ZONE

RED LINE

OTHER RINKS

International hockey, such as in the Olympics, is played on ice surfaces larger than NHL rinks. Olympic ice is 200 feet (61 m) long and 100 feet (30 m) wide. Many college teams in the United States also play on international-sized ice. The extra space on the rink often favors the game's better skaters.

200 FEET LONG

FACE-OFF CIRCLE

BLUE LINE

GOAL

GOAL LINE

BOARDS

75 FEET

4 FEET

6 FEET

POSITIONS

When teams are playing at full strength, each team has six players on the ice: three forwards (center, left wing, right wing), two defensemen, and a goaltender.

TRIVIA

Name that Position!

Can you match the position of each of the hockey players?

1. _____

2. _____

2. _____

3. _____

4. _____

5. _____

POSITIONS

CENTER

LEFT WING

RIGHT WING

DEFENSEMAN

GOALTENDER

PENALTY PUNISHMENT

A player who commits a serious penalty, such as trying to injure another player, is immediately ejected from the game. When players are called for other penalties, such as hooking, charging, or slashing, they must leave the rink and sit in the penalty box for two, four, or five minutes. While they are in the box, their teammates must play short-handed. The short-handed team may have three or four skaters and a goalie on the ice while the other team is on the power play. Teams play short-handed until the penalty time ends or until the opponent scores a goal. Sometimes players on opposite teams get called for penalties at about the same time. Then the teams each play with four skaters and a goalie. Teams put a lot of practice into their power play and short-handed units, which are called special teams.

5. _____ **2.** _____

1. _____

4. _____

3. _____ **2.** _____

FACT:

If a team is down by a goal with only a few minutes remaining in the game, the coach may decide to pull the goalie off the ice. In the goalie's place, the coach can add another skater. Although it leaves the net wide open, it gives the team a 6-on-5 advantage and a better chance to score a goal.

Answer: 1. goaltender 2. defenseman 3. left wing 4. center 5. right wing

EQUIPMENT

When hockey was first played in the late 1800s, players only used a pair of skates and a stick. Over time protective gear was added, including padding and hard plastic for shins, knees, shoulders, and elbows. It took awhile for players, especially at the professional level, to get used to wearing helmets and masks.

The first NHL goalie to wear a mask was Jacques Plante. After getting his face bloodied by a puck in a 1959 game, Plante got stitched up and returned to the game with a mask. He continued to wear a mask, even though his coach didn't approve. Then more goalies started wearing masks. Andy Brown of the Pittsburgh Penguins was the last goalie to play in a game without a mask, in 1974.

In 1979 the NHL required all of the draft picks from that year forward to wear helmets. The league allowed players already in the league to play without headgear. One of the players, 1978 draft pick Craig MacTavish, played without a helmet until he retired in 1997—18 years after the helmet rule was first enforced.

Many NHL players wear helmets without face protection. Some wear a plastic eye shield, while younger players have full shields or metal cages.

JACQUES PLANTE, MONTREAL CANADIENS

HELMET

EYE SHIELD

MOUTHGUARD

SHOULDER PADS

JERSEY

ELBOW PADS

HOCKEY PANTS
(BREEZERS)

GLOVES

SHIN PADS

SKATES

STICKS **ALL AROUND**

Players pass and shoot the puck with hockey sticks.
The sticks come in various lengths and are chosen
according to the player's size. They have a curved
blade at the bottom to control the puck. In the early
days hockey sticks were made of wood and had a
flat blade. Today most sticks are made of high-tech,
composite materials that make them lighter and
stronger. Some of the top players can use the sticks
to fire shots that go more than 100 mph.

STICK

UNIFORMS

Football has helmets and baseball has caps, but hockey teams are defined by their jerseys. The New York Rangers have been known as the Blueshirts since their early days. The St. Louis Blues are nicknamed the "Blue Notes" because of the big, blue-winged musical note that graces the front of their jerseys.

DRESSED FOR SUCCESS ||||||||||||||||||||||||||||||||||||

So what are the best uniforms in the NHL? Ask 30 fans and you might get 30 different answers. Here are a few that have gotten rave reviews over the years—as well as a couple that have caused critics to hold their noses. The Penguins, like Pittsburgh's other professional sports teams, wear black, yellow, and white. But originally they wore light blue sweaters. In recent years the team has occasionally brought back the powder blues. One of those times was for the Winter Classic, a pro game played in an outdoor arena.

THE GOOD

The Montreal Canadiens are one of the NHL's original teams. The team has worn similar red, white, and blue jerseys since the league started in 1917. Their "CH" logo is instantly recognizable. It stands for the team's official French name, Le Club de Hockey Canadien. (French is the official language of the Canadian province of Quebec.)

Many NHL jerseys feature several colors, but not the Detroit Red Wings' jerseys. They keep it simple and classy with red and white. The jerseys have one of the sport's most unique logos—the winged wheel—across the chest. Other teams have followed the Wings with their own feathered logos, including the Blues and the Flyers.

THE UGLY

Critics cried foul when the New York Islanders tried to change the jerseys that won four straight Stanley Cups. The logo featured a salty fisherman who looked like the character on a box of frozen seafood. When the Isles skated onto the ice to play their rivals—the New York Rangers—opposing fans repeatedly chanted, "We want fish sticks!" The Islanders returned to their classic jerseys in 1984 after one season.

THE BAD

It has taken years for the Vancouver Canucks to perfect their uniforms. While their current blue, green, and white sweaters end up on best-of lists, earlier sweaters were hard on the eyes. With black, orange, and yellow as their official colors, the Canucks once sported a giant V that stretched from the player's shoulders to his belly button.

KEEPING WARM

Do you know why hockey jerseys are sometimes called sweaters? The first hockey teams wore warm, wool, knitted sweaters when they played on outdoor ice rinks in the middle of cold winters. As games moved into indoor rinks, players wanted jerseys made out of lighter materials.

CHAPTER 2

THE TEAMS

For many years there were only six teams in the NHL: the Boston Bruins, Chicago Blackhawks, Detroit Red Wings, Montreal Canadiens, New York Rangers, and Toronto Maple Leafs. In 1967 the league doubled in size. Over the next 33 years, 18 more teams joined the league, putting pro hockey in almost every major city in North America.

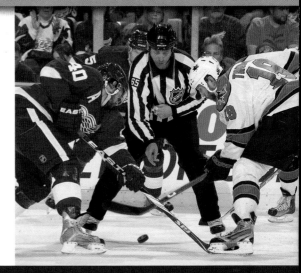

EASTERN CONFERENCE

Atlantic Division

New Jersey Devils—The Devils started out in Kansas City as the Scouts before moving to Colorado as the Rockies and finally to New Jersey.

New York Islanders—The Islanders' Mike Bossy had nine 50-goal seasons for New York; he is the only player in history to have that many with the same team.

New York Rangers—The Rangers were not the first NHL team to play in New York City, but they survived after the New York/Brooklyn Americans folded.

Philadelphia Flyers—The NHL doubled in size, going from six teams to 12 in 1967. In 1974 the Flyers became the first of those new teams to win the Stanley Cup.

Pittsburgh Penguins—When Mario Lemieux came out of retirement in 2000, he became the first team owner to skate in an NHL game.

Southeast Division

Atlanta Thrashers—The Thrashers are the second NHL team to play in Atlanta; the Flames spent eight seasons there before moving to Calgary, Alberta.

Carolina Hurricanes—In 1997 the Hurricanes moved from Hartford, Connecticut—where they were the Whalers—to Raleigh, North Carolina.

Florida Panthers—The Panthers won 33 games during their first season (1993–1994) in Florida, a record for an expansion team.

Tampa Bay Lightning—When they won the 2004 Cup, the Lightning became the southern-most team in the NHL to win a championship.

Washington Capitals—The Capitals' first season, 1974–1975, was the worst for any team in NHL history; they had a .131 winning percentage and lost 17 games in a row during one stretch.

Northeast Division

Boston Bruins—The Bruins were the first U.S. team to join the NHL, which only had Canadian teams at the time.

Buffalo Sabres—The NHL decided to expand into Buffalo, New York, in 1970; the decision was based on the success of a minor-league team that played in that city for 30 years and won five championships.

Montreal Canadiens—Only Major League Baseball's New York Yankees have won more professional championships (27) than the Canadiens, who have 24 Stanley Cups.

Ottawa Senators—The original Ottawa Senators existed from the late 1800s to 1935. In 1992 the NHL added a new team with the old name in Canada's capital city.

Toronto Maple Leafs—The Leafs were first called the Arenas and the St. Patricks before they got their current nickname in 1926.

Central Division

Chicago Blackhawks—In 1937–1938 the Blackhawks went 14–25–9, yet won the Stanley Cup; it remains the worst record of any championship team.

Columbus Blue Jackets—The Blue Jackets became Ohio's second NHL team when they joined the league in 2000; the Cleveland Barons lasted just two seasons before the franchise moved in the 1970s.

Detroit Red Wings—Detroit's NHL team was called the Cougars for four years and then the Falcons for two years before settling on the Red Wings in 1932.

Nashville Predators—The Predators got their nickname because the bones of a saber-toothed tiger were found in an underground cave near Nashville, Tennessee.

St. Louis Blues—The Blues played in the Stanley Cup finals in each of their first three seasons, losing to the Canadiens in 1968 and 1969 and the Bruins in 1970.

Pacific Division

Anaheim Ducks—The team was originally called the Mighty Ducks, named after a 1992 Disney movie about a youth hockey team.

Dallas Stars—Mike Modano spent 20 seasons with the Stars—four when the team was in Minnesota—and became the NHL's top-scoring U.S.-born player.

Los Angeles Kings—The Kings pulled off "the trade of the century" on August 9, 1988, when the team got Wayne Gretzky from the Edmonton Oilers.

Phoenix Coyotes—Phoenix is one of many teams with a connection to Wayne Gretzky; he coached the Coyotes for four seasons and was once a partial owner of the Arizona team.

San Jose Sharks—The Sharks aren't the first NHL team to play in California's San Francisco Bay area; the Oakland Seals were part of the 1967 expansion class but lasted just nine years.

Northwest Division

Calgary Flames—Three brothers from the Sutter family have coached the Flames: Brent, Brian, and Darryl; another brother—Ron Sutter—played for Calgary, as did Darryl's son, Brett.

Colorado Avalanche—The Avalanche won the Stanley Cup in 1995–1996, their first year in Denver after moving from Quebec City, where they were the Nordiques.

Edmonton Oilers—During the Wayne Gretzky-led dynasty of the 1980s, the Oilers scored at least 400 goals five seasons in a row.

Minnesota Wild—Before the first home game in franchise history, the Wild retired the number 1 in honor of their fans, who were without an NHL team for seven years.

Vancouver Canucks—The Canucks are still waiting for their first Stanley Cup, but the city of Vancouver isn't; in 1915 a team called the Vancouver Millionaires won the trophy.

TRIVIA

Name the seven NHL teams whose nicknames are animals.

Answer: Bruins (a bear), Coyotes, Ducks, Panthers, Penguins, Sharks, Thrashers (a bird)

CHAMPIONS

Since the late 1800s, hockey teams have competed for the Stanley Cup, which goes to the sport's champion every year. The NHL was created in 1917, and the famous trophy became the ultimate prize for teams in the world's best hockey league. No team captured more Cups than the Montreal Canadiens, who have won it an amazing 24 times, including once before the NHL even existed.

STANLEY CUP CHAMPIONS

TEAM	YEARS WON
Montreal Canadiens	1916, 1924, 1930, 1931, 1944, 1946, 1953, 1956, 1957, 1958, 1959, 1960, 1965, 1966, 1968, 1969, 1971, 1973, 1976, 1977, 1978, 1979, 1986, 1993
Toronto Maple Leafs	1918, 1922, 1932, 1942, 1945, 1947, 1948, 1949, 1951, 1962, 1963, 1964, 1967
Detroit Red Wings	1936, 1937, 1943, 1950, 1952, 1954, 1955, 1997, 1998, 2002, 2008
Boston Bruins	1929, 1939, 1941, 1970, 1972
Edmonton Oilers	1984, 1985, 1987, 1988, 1990
Chicago Blackhawks	1934, 1938, 1961, 2010
New York Rangers	1928, 1933, 1940, 1994
New York Islanders	1980, 1981, 1982, 1983
New Jersey Devils	1995, 2000, 2003
Pittsburgh Penguins	1991, 1992, 2009

Colorado Avalanche	1996, 2001	Philadelphia Flyers	1974, 1975
Calgary Flames	1989	Carolina Hurricanes	2006
Dallas Stars	1999	Tampa Bay Lightning	2004

OTHER STANLEY CUP WINNERS—NHL ERA

Ottawa Senators	1921, 1923, 1927	Montreal Maroons	1926, 1935

OTHER STANLEY CUP WINNERS—PRE-NHL

Ottawa Silver Screen	1903*, 1904, 1905, 1906*
Montreal AAA	1893, 1894, 1902*, 1903*
Montreal Victorias	1895, 1896*, 1897, 1898, 1899*
Montreal Wanderers	1906*, 1907*, 1908, 1910

Winnipeg Victorias	1896*, 1901, 1902*	Montreal Shamrocks	1899*, 1900
Ottawa Senators	1909, 1911	Quebec Bulldogs	1912, 1913
Kenora Thistles	1907*	Seattle Metropolitans	1917
Toronto Blueshirts	1914	Vancouver Millionaires	1915

*Years the Stanley Cup was shared by leagues

THE MONTREAL AMATEUR ATHLETIC ASSOCIATION (AAA)

DYNASTIES

Every so often a team becomes so good that it dominates for several years in a row. Those eras are known as dynasties. The NHL recognizes nine dynasties throughout its history. Five franchises have made up those dynasties.

NEW YORK ISLANDERS

From 1979 to 1983, the Islanders made NHL history. They became the first franchise from the United States to win four straight Stanley Cups. Their first championship took place eight years after the team was added to the NHL. Seven Hall of Famers, including coach Al Arbour, were part of the historic teams, which had a 16–3 finals record.

TORONTO MAPLE LEAFS

The Maple Leafs captured four Stanley Cups, including three in a row, between 1946 and 1951. Thirteen Hall of Famers, including president Conn Smythe, were part of the Toronto team during that stretch. The Maple Leafs made another great run in the 1960s. They won four more Cups between 1961 and 1967. Sixteen Hall of Famers helped make the second Leafs dynasty possible.

MONTREAL CANADIENS

The Canadiens have won more Stanley Cups than any other team. They also put together three dynasties: 1956–1960, 1964–1969, and 1975–1979. Montreal's first dynasty included five consecutive Cup wins. Twelve players from that era are now in the Hall of Fame. The second dynasty included four more titles and many of the same players. The final dynasty won four Stanley Cups in a row and featured 11 Hall of Famers.

KEN DRYDEN

OTTAWA SENATORS

The Ottawa dynasty rose to power as the original Senators. Between 1919 and 1927, the Senators became the NHL's first dynasty. They won four Stanley Cups behind 14 future Hall of Famers. One of those players, King Clancy, played every position on the ice— including goaltender—during a 1923 Cup finals game.

EDMONTON OILERS

Edmonton Oilers center Wayne Gretzky

Having the great Wayne Gretzky was a big reason why the Oilers were a dynasty from 1983 to 1990. But Edmonton had so much more. In fact, when Edmonton won its fifth championship during the run, Gretzky had already been traded to the Los Angeles Kings. During both the 1983–1984 and the 1985–1986 seasons, the Oilers had three players with 50 goals or more and four players with 100 points or more. Six Hall of Famers led Edmonton on its great run.

GREATEST SEASONS

Each season one team stands tall after a grueling regular season and a hard-fought playoffs. With the Stanley Cup hoisted high, the players skate around the rink as NHL champions. But there are only a few teams that have had truly historic seasons. From star players to masterful coaching, these teams set NHL records that still stand today. It's easy to see why these teams are considered the greatest of all time.

MOST POINTS: 1976-1977 MONTREAL CANADIENS

During their 1970s dynasty, the Montreal Canadiens compiled one of the best seasons in NHL history. In 1976–1977 they went 60–8–12. They ended with a record 132 points for the regular-season standings (two points for wins, one point for ties). Right wing Guy Lafleur scored 56 goals and had 136 points, and Steve Shutt scored 60 goals. The Canadiens scored 216 more goals than their opponents. Montreal cruised through the playoffs, losing just twice and sweeping the Boston Bruins in the finals for its 20th Stanley Cup.

HIGHEST-SCORING TEAM: 1983-1984 EDMONTON OILERS

The 1983–1984 Oilers team was a well-oiled scoring machine. The first year they won a Stanley Cup, they set a scoring record with 446 goals—an average of more than 5.5 goals per game. Wayne Gretzky led the way with 87 goals and 205 points. Glenn Anderson and Jari Kurri scored more than 50 goals each. Kurri, Mark Messier, and defenseman Paul Coffey each had more than 100 points.

MOST WINS: 1995-1996 DETROIT RED WINGS

In 1995–1996 the Detroit Red Wings were dominant during the regular season, winning a record 62 games. They were led by top-scorer Sergei Fedorov, who had 107 points, and longtime captain Steve Yzerman, who had 95 points. Coach Scotty Bowman, who also coached the 1976–1977 Canadiens, was behind the bench. Detroit won the President's Trophy as the team with the best regular-season record. However, their great season was spoiled when they failed to win the Stanley Cup.

BEST WIN PERCENTAGE: 1929-1930 BOSTON BRUINS

In the 1920s and 1930, NHL teams played only 44 games in a season compared to 82 today. In 1929–1930 the Boston Bruins had what still stands as the league's record-best winning percentage. Behind great defenseman Eddie Shore, the team went 38–5–1 for a .875 success rate. Although the Bruins won the Stanley Cup a year earlier, they were unable to repeat in 1929–1930.

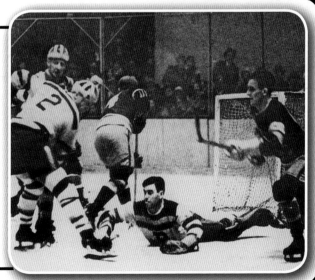

COACHES

They are known as the bench bosses, the ringmasters, and the geniuses behind the game. Coaches have the task of putting the right line combinations together, selecting the best goalies, and motivating their teams to play to their full potential.

SCOTTY BOWMAN

Scotty Bowman deserves a spot at the top of the list of greatest hockey coaches. He coached for 30 seasons and won 1,244 games—462 more victories than Al Arbour, the second coach on the list. Bowman won nine Stanley Cup championships—five with the Canadiens, three with the Red Wings, and one with the Penguins. Bowman won his first Stanley Cup in 1973 and his last in 2002.

AL ARBOUR

It didn't take long for the New York Islanders to go from an expansion team to an NHL dynasty. Coach Al Arbour is a big reason why. The coach took over the team in 1973, one year after the Islanders were created. By the end of the 1979–1980 season, they were Stanley Cup champions. New York also won the next three Cups behind Arbour. In 23 seasons Arbour compiled 782 wins, good enough for second on the all-time wins list.

HERB BROOKS

One of the great coaching jobs of all time didn't take place in the NHL. Although Herb Brooks coached in the NHL for seven seasons and had only two losing seasons, his triumphant moment came during the 1980 Olympics. He led Team USA to the greatest upset in sports history. During the "Miracle on Ice" the Americans defeated the mighty Soviet Union team in Lake Placid, New York. A master motivator, Brooks also won three college titles at the University of Minnesota.

Top Coaches

- Jack Adams, Red Wings/Cougars/Falcons—coach of the year trophy is named after the three-time Cup winner
- Al Arbour, Blues/Islanders—led Isles dynasty that won four championships in a row
- Toe Blake, Canadiens—won eight Cups with Montreal, including five in a row
- Scotty Bowman, Blues/Canadiens/Sabres/Penguins/Red Wings—won nine Stanley Cups, more than any other coach
- Herb Brooks, Rangers/North Stars/Devils/Penguins—coached the gold medal-winning 1980 U.S. Olympic hockey team
- Hap Day, Maple Leafs—led Toronto to five Cup victories
- Punch Imlach, Maple Leafs/Sabres—oversaw the Leafs' second dynasty, winning four titles
- Dick Irvin, Blackhawks/Maple Leafs/Canadiens—won four Stanley Cups
- Mike Keenan, Flyers/Blackhawks/Rangers/Blues/ Canucks/Bruins/Panthers/Flames—ranks fifth in all-time wins
- Glen Sather, Oilers/Rangers—won four championships with Edmonton dynasty

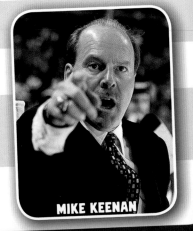

MIKE KEENAN

CHAPTER 3 PLAYERS

FORWARDS

Forwards skate up front and get down deep. These right wings, left wings, and centers are the driving force behind putting points on the scoreboard. If the forwards don't start the offense, they usually finish it with nifty passes and gritty goals.

WAYNE GRETZKY

Wayne Gretzky's records will likely stand for a long time. "The Great One" was the only player to score more than 200 points in a single season—a feat he accomplished four times. His best season was 1985–1986 when he scored 52 goals and had 163 assists for 215 points. In 1981–1982 he scored a record 92 goals. For his career, Gretzky recorded 2,857 points, but his 1,963 assists alone would put him at the top of the all-time scoring list. The NHL retired Gretzky's 99 jersey number, meaning no player from any team can wear the number.

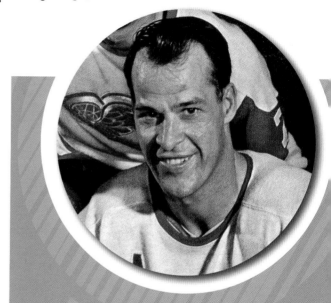

GORDIE HOWE

Gordie Howe was called Mr. Hockey for a good reason. He led the NHL in points six times, but he was also known for his rough-and-tumble play. Any player who scores a goal, gets an assist, and gets in a fight achieves a "Gordie Howe hat trick." Howe played professional hockey until 1980 at age 51. During his final three seasons, he played for the New England Whalers along with his sons, Mark and Marty. In 1997, when Howe was 69 years old, the Detroit Vipers of the International Hockey League signed him to play in one game, making Howe the first professional hockey player to play in six different decades.

MARIO LEMIEUX

Who knows how many points "Super" Mario Lemieux would have scored had he been healthy for his entire career. Still, a battle with cancer and back surgery couldn't keep the Pittsburgh star sidelined for good. Three years after retiring, being inducted into the Hall of Fame, and becoming part-owner of the Penguins, he made a comeback and played five more seasons for Pittsburgh. Lemieux is the only person in history to win a Stanley Cup as a player and as an owner.

Top Forwards

- Jean Beliveau, Canadiens—named to 13 All-Star Games
- Wayne Gretzky, Oilers/Kings/Blues/Rangers—hockey's all-time leading scorer
- Gordie Howe, Red Wings/Houston Aeros/Whalers—played 32 seasons of professional hockey
- Bobby Hull, Blackhawks/Jets/Whalers—four-time MVP (two in NHL, two in the World Hockey Association)
- Guy Lafleur, Canadiens/Rangers/Nordiques—two-time MVP
- Mario Lemieux, Penguins—won three MVP awards
- Mark Messier, Oilers/Rangers/Canucks/Indianapolis Racers/Stingers—named to 15 All-Star Games
- Stan Mikita, Blackhawks—four-time scoring leader
- Howie Morenz, Canadiens/Blackhawks/Rangers—three-time MVP
- Maurice Richard, Canadiens—led Montreal to eight Stanley Cup wins

JEAN BELIVEAU

GUY LAFLEUR

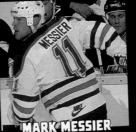

MARK MESSIER

MAURICE RICHARD

DEFENSEMEN

They're known as the blue liners and are often the last line of defense before the goaltender. But defensemen do much more than take on the other team's forwards. The best defenders can score too.

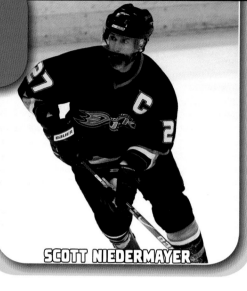

SCOTT NIEDERMAYER

BOBBY ORR

Bobby Orr changed the defenseman position forever in the NHL. There were offensive defensemen before Orr, but few could skate or handle the puck like him. During one penalty kill, he skated for 21 seconds without losing the puck before scoring a short-handed goal. He was named the NHL's MVP three times in his career.

CHRIS CHELIOS

You can't keep Chris Chelios down. After playing more than 24 seasons in the NHL, he played minor-league hockey from 2008 to 2010. Then the NHL called him one more time. In 2009–2010, at the age of 48, he played seven games for the Atlanta Thrashers before retiring in August. No defenseman has played in more NHL games than Chelios. In fact, only three other players—all forwards—have played more

DOUG HARVEY

Doug Harvey was a big reason why the Montreal Canadiens won five Stanley Cups in a row from 1956–1960. He was a great defender who blocked shots and moved the puck out of his team's end. He also excelled on power plays and passing the puck to his high-scoring teammates. Harvey won the Norris Trophy as the NHL's best defenseman seven times. Only Bobby Orr has won the award more times.

Top Defensemen

- Ray Bourque, Bruins/Avalanche—voted to 19 All-Star Games
- Chris Chelios, Canadiens/Blackhawks/Red Wings/Thrashers—played 26 seasons in the league
- Paul Coffey, Oilers/Penguins/Kings/Red Wings/Whalers/Flyers/Blackhawks/Hurricanes/Bruins—ranks second among defensemen in career goals (396)
- Doug Harvey, Canadiens/Rangers/Red Wings/Blues—13-time All-Star Game pick
- Red Kelly, Red Wings/Maple Leafs—selected for the All-Star Game 12 times
- Nicklas Lidstrom, Red Wings—points leader (1,050) among active blue liners
- Bobby Orr, Bruins/Blackhawks—named NHL's best defenseman eight times
- Denis Potvin, Islanders—named league's best defenseman three times
- Larry Robinson, Canadiens/Kings—twice named league's best defenseman
- Eddie Shore, Bruins/New York Americans—four-time MVP

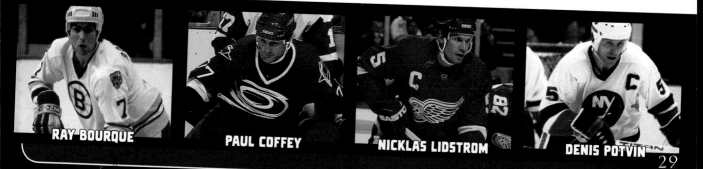

RAY BOURQUE   PAUL COFFEY   NICKLAS LIDSTROM   DENIS POTVIN

GOALTENDERS

Goaltenders play one of the toughest positions in any sport. They need eagle eyes and catlike reflexes to stop speedy slap shots, wicked wristers, and tricky tip-ins.

ROBERT LUONGO

PATRICK ROY

You couldn't script a better full first season than the one Patrick Roy had. By the time the 1986 playoffs started during his rookie year, he was the Canadiens' number one goalie. He led the team all the way to the Stanley Cup championship. He allowed fewer than two goals per game during the playoffs and won the Conn Smythe Award as the playoff MVP. Over the next 17 seasons, "St. Patrick" won three more titles—one with Montreal and two with the Colorado Avalanche.

MARTIN BRODEUR

Patrick Roy's records seemed unbreakable when he retired in 2003, but Martin Brodeur proved he was up to the task. Drafted in 1990, he has spent his entire career with the New Jersey Devils and continues to play. He has won three Stanley Cups and owns some of the game's most spectacular saves with his unique defensive style. Brodeur has more wins (602) and more shutouts (110) than any other goalie in league history.

JACQUES PLANTE

Jacques Plante's influence on the game is still felt today. He was the first NHL goaltender to regularly wear a mask to protect his face from flying pucks, although others had tried it briefly. Even though his coach didn't like the look at first, Plante kept the mask as the Canadiens won 18 games in a row. He won six Stanley Cups and was one of the few goaltenders to win the Hart Trophy as league MVP.

Top Goaltenders

- Turk Broda, Maple Leafs—led Toronto to five championships
- Martin Brodeur, Devils—owns most of the NHL's career goalie records
- Ken Dryden, Canadiens—won six Stanley Cups in eight-year career
- Bill Durnan, Canadiens—voted NHL's top goalie six times
- George Hainsworth, Canadiens/Maple Leafs—voted league's best goalie three times
- Dominik Hasek, Blackhawks/Sabres/Red Wings/Senators—only goalie to win two MVPs
- Jacques Plante, Canadiens/Rangers/Blues/Maple Leafs/Bruins/Oilers— led Montreal to five Cup wins in a row
- Patrick Roy, Canadiens/Avalanche—playoff MVP in three of his four Stanley Cup wins
- Terry Sawchuk, Red Wings/Bruins/Maple Leafs/Kings/Rangers—voted top goalie four times

MARTIN BRODEUR

KEN DRYDEN

DOMINIK HASEK

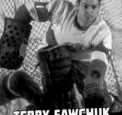
TERRY SAWCHUK

CURRENT & RISING STARS

The NHL has had a legendary past, but it also has a bright future. The league currently has several players striving for the Hall of Fame. From Joe Thornton to Sidney Crosby, these stars add an exciting spark to pro hockey.

SIDNEY CROSBY

Few players have burst onto the hockey scene like Pittsburgh Penguins star Sidney Crosby. "Sid the Kid" was only 19 years old when he was named the team captain—the youngest captain in NHL history. He also became the league's youngest scoring champion and the second-youngest MVP after Wayne Gretzky. In 2009 he became the youngest captain of a Stanley Cup-winning team.

ALEX OVECHKIN

It didn't take long for Alex Ovechkin to become a superstar. In 2006 the Russian left wing won the Calder Trophy as rookie of the year. Two seasons later he was the league MVP, winning the first of back-to-back Hart Trophies. He scored 50 or more goals and more than 100 points in four of his first five seasons. Wayne Gretzky and Mario Lemieux are the only other players in league history to have 200 goals and 200 assists through their first four seasons.

HENRIK AND DANIEL SEDIN

Two of the best players in the NHL are twin brothers Henrik (left) and Daniel Sedin of the Vancouver Canucks. In 1999 the Canucks made a trade to get the second- and third-overall picks in the summer draft and took the Sedin twins. Through their first nine seasons, Daniel has 208 goals and 547 points, and Henrik has 138 goals and 572 points. In 2010 Henrik led the NHL with 83 assists and 112 points.

Top Current & Rising Stars

- Sidney Crosby, F, Penguins—scored 120 points during his second season in the NHL

- Jarome Iginla, F, Flames—two-time league leader in goals

- Patrick Kane, F, Blackhawks—2008 rookie of the year

- Evgeni Malkin, F, Penguins—2007 rookie of the year and 2009 playoff MVP

- Ryan Miller, G, Sabres—MVP of 2010 Olympic hockey tournament

- Rick Nash, F, Blue Jackets—has been selected to the All-Star Game four times

- Alex Ovechkin, F, Capitals—two-time MVP scored 50-plus goals in four of his first five seasons

- Zach Parise, F, Devils—scored 94 points in 2008-2009

- Henrik Sedin, F, Canucks—NHL's scoring leader with 112 points in 2009-2010

- Joe Thornton, F, Bruins/Sharks—won the MVP in 2006

JAROME IGINLA   EVGENI MALKIN   RYAN MILLER   RICK NASH

MVPS

After every season the NHL awards the Hart Trophy to the season's best player. It is the league's most valuable player award, and it has gone to some great hockey stars.

TRADED AWAY

During the 2005–2006 season, the Boston Bruins sent Joe Thornton all the way across the country, trading him to the San Jose Sharks. Thornton joined a team that was 8–12–4 and had lost 10 games in a row. But he led the Sharks to a 36–15–7 record the rest of the way. Thornton was the only player in NHL history to be traded during the season in which he won the MVP.

GREATNESS HAS HART

The great Wayne Gretzky won nine Hart Trophies, including an amazing eight in a row from 1980 to 1987 with the Edmonton Oilers. In 1989, after "the trade of the century" sent Gretzky to the Kings, he won his final MVP award. Mario Lemieux broke up Gretzky's streak after a 168-point season in 1988–1989, winning the first of his three Hart Trophies.

GOALIES ARE VALUABLE TOO

Goaltenders have their own postseason awards, but they have also been voted as the MVP seven times in NHL history. The first goalie to receive the award was the New York Americans' Roy Worters in 1929. In 1997 the Sabres' Dominik Hasek became the first goalie since Jacques Plante in 1962 to be named MVP. He won the award again the following year, becoming the only goalie to win the award twice. The most recent goalie to win the award was the Canadiens' Jose Theodore in 2002.

MULTIPLE MVP WINNERS

Player	Team	Awards
Wayne Gretzky	Oilers/Kings	9
Gordie Howe	Red Wings	6
Eddie Shore	Bruins	4
Bobby Clarke	Flyers	3
Mario Lemieux	Penguins	3
Howie Morenz	Canadiens	3
Bobby Orr	Bruins	3
Jean Beliveau	Canadiens	2
Bill Cowley	Bruins	2
Phil Esposito	Bruins	2
Bobby Hull	Blackhawks/Blues	2
Guy Lafleur	Canadiens	2
Mark Messier	Rangers/Oilers	2
Stan Mikita	Blackhawks	2
Alex Ovechkin	Capitals	2
Nels Stewart	Maroons	2

DREAM TEAM

Imagine a team made up of the greatest players who ever skated onto a hockey rink. Few would argue that Wayne Gretzky should be the number one center. But from there picking the lineup would be almost impossible. Is Martin Brodeur the best goalie, or is Patrick Roy? How do you choose between Nicklas Lidstrom and Chris Chelios on defense? Is Bobby Hull the best left wing of all time? Is Brett Hull the best right wing?

Most hockey teams play with four forward lines consisting of a center, left wing, and right wing, three defensive pairs, and up to three goalies.

IF YOU WERE THE COACH, WHO WOULD YOU PICK FOR YOUR TEAM?

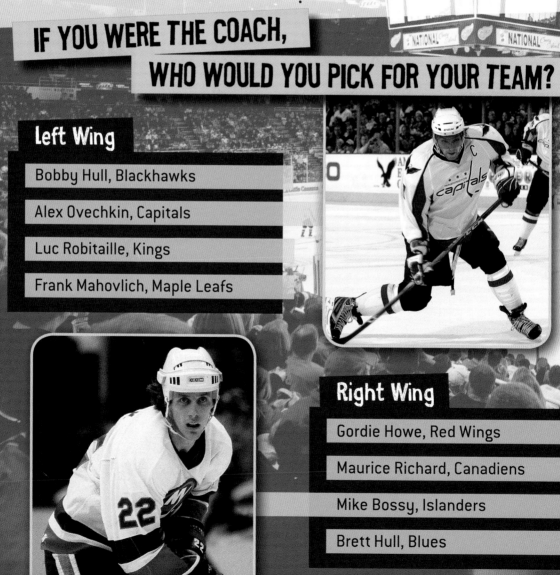

Left Wing

Bobby Hull, Blackhawks

Alex Ovechkin, Capitals

Luc Robitaille, Kings

Frank Mahovlich, Maple Leafs

Right Wing

Gordie Howe, Red Wings

Maurice Richard, Canadiens

Mike Bossy, Islanders

Brett Hull, Blues

Center

Wayne Gretzky, Oilers

Mario Lemieux, Penguins

Mark Messier, Oilers

Jean Beliveau, Canadiens

Goaltender

Patrick Roy, Avalanche

Martin Brodeur, Devils

Terry Sawchuk, Red Wings

Defensemen

Bobby Orr, Bruins

Doug Harvey, Canadiens

Ray Bourque, Bruins

Nicklas Lidstrom, Red Wings

Eddie Shore, Bruins

Denis Potvin, Islanders

CURRENT VS. CLASSIC

What was the best era of the NHL? The days when only the Original Six teams existed? The rough-and-tough days of the 1970s? Are we seeing it today? Can you even compare various periods of the NHL? Look at some of today's stars matched up against some of yesterday's best. Who do you think is better?

LEFT WING

Alex Ovechkin, Capitals	Bobby Hull, Blackhawks/ Jets/Whalers*
6 feet 2 inches (188 cm) 223 pounds (101 kg)	5 feet 10 inches (178 cm) 195 pounds (88 kg)
2005–present	1957–1980
269 goals 260 assists 529 points 305 penalty minutes	913 goals 895 assists 1,808 points 823 penalty minutes

RIGHT WING

Jarome Iginla, Flames	Gordie Howe, Red Wings/ Aeros/Whalers*
6 feet 1 inch (185 cm) 207 pounds (94 kg)	6 feet (183 cm) 205 pounds (93 kg)
1996–present	1946–1980
441 goals 479 assists 920 points 726 penalty minutes	975 goals 1,383 assists 2,358 points 2,084 penalty minutes

JAROME IGINLA

All stats are through the 2009–2010 season.

CENTER

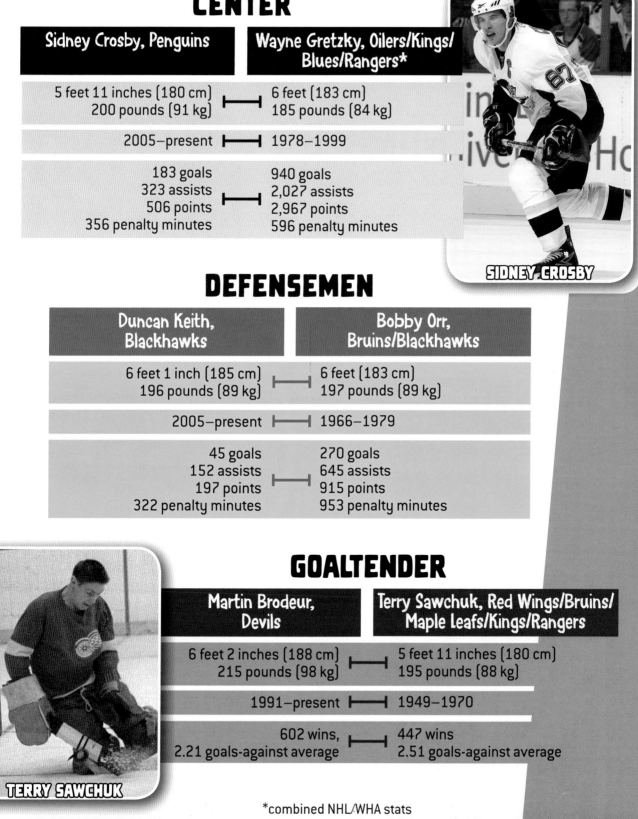

Sidney Crosby, Penguins	Wayne Gretzky, Oilers/Kings/Blues/Rangers*
5 feet 11 inches (180 cm) 200 pounds (91 kg)	6 feet (183 cm) 185 pounds (84 kg)
2005–present	1978–1999
183 goals 323 assists 506 points 356 penalty minutes	940 goals 2,027 assists 2,967 points 596 penalty minutes

SIDNEY CROSBY

DEFENSEMEN

Duncan Keith, Blackhawks	Bobby Orr, Bruins/Blackhawks
6 feet 1 inch (185 cm) 196 pounds (89 kg)	6 feet (183 cm) 197 pounds (89 kg)
2005–present	1966–1979
45 goals 152 assists 197 points 322 penalty minutes	270 goals 645 assists 915 points 953 penalty minutes

GOALTENDER

TERRY SAWCHUK

Martin Brodeur, Devils	Terry Sawchuk, Red Wings/Bruins/Maple Leafs/Kings/Rangers
6 feet 2 inches (188 cm) 215 pounds (98 kg)	5 feet 11 inches (180 cm) 195 pounds (88 kg)
1991–present	1949–1970
602 wins, 2.21 goals-against average	447 wins 2.51 goals-against average

*combined NHL/WHA stats

CHAPTER 4

GREATEST MOMENTS

LUCKY NUMBER 7

There are few sporting events as thrilling as a Game 7 of the Stanley Cup Finals. There have been 15 times in NHL history where the championship was decided in Game 7. The latest occurred in 2009, when Sidney Crosby, Evgeni Malkin, and the Pittsburgh Penguins beat the Detroit Red Wings in an exciting matchup.

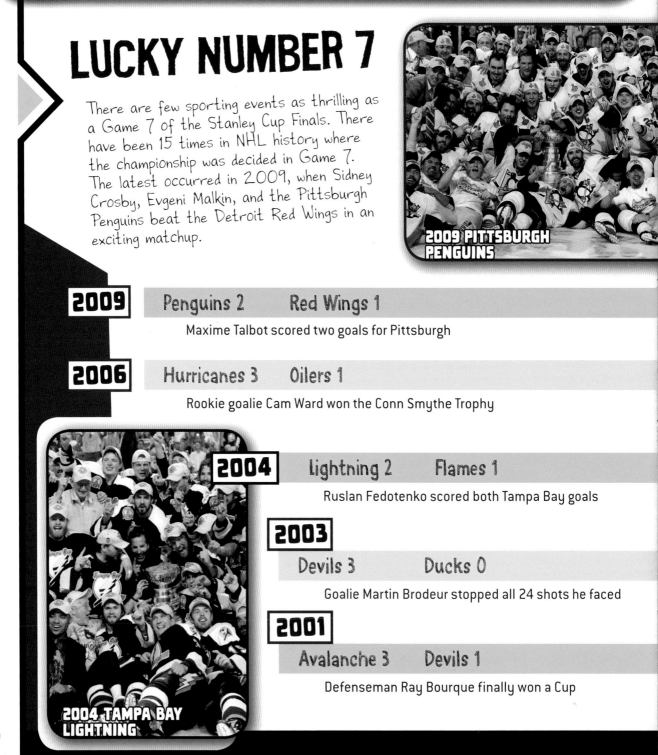

2009 PITTSBURGH PENGUINS

2009	Penguins 2	Red Wings 1

Maxime Talbot scored two goals for Pittsburgh

2006	Hurricanes 3	Oilers 1

Rookie goalie Cam Ward won the Conn Smythe Trophy

2004	Lightning 2	Flames 1

Ruslan Fedotenko scored both Tampa Bay goals

2003	Devils 3	Ducks 0

Goalie Martin Brodeur stopped all 24 shots he faced

2001	Avalanche 3	Devils 1

Defenseman Ray Bourque finally won a Cup

2004 TAMPA BAY LIGHTNING

1994 Rangers 3   Canucks 2

Mark Messier helped New York end a 54-year title drought

1987 Oilers 3   Flyers 1

Part of Edmonton's dynasty

2006 CAROLINA HURRICANES

1971 Canadiens 3   Blackhawks 2

Rookie goalie Ken Dryden was the playoff MVP

1965

Canadiens 4   Blackhawks 0

Gump Worsley made 20 saves to shut out Chicago

1964

Maple Leafs 4   Red Wings 0

Johnny Bower made 33 saves in the shutout

2003 NEW JERSEY DEVILS

1955

Red Wings 3   Canadiens 1

Alex Delvecchio scored two goals for the winners

1954 Red Wings 2   Canadiens 1   OT

The second and most recent Game 7 to go to overtime

1950 Red Wings 4   Rangers 3   2 OT

The first Game 7 to go to overtime

1945 Maple Leafs 2   Red Wings 1

Defenseman Babe Pratt scored the game-winning goal

1942 Maple Leafs 3   Red Wings 1

Toronto erased a 3-games-to-0 deficit in the series

2001 COLORADO AVALANCHE

LONGEST GAMES

One of the reasons playoff hockey games are so exciting is the chance for extended overtime. During the regular season, there is only one overtime before the teams have a shootout. In a shootout, each team has five chances for one of its players to shoot a goal one-on-one with the goalie. The team with the most goals in the shootout wins.

After the regular season ends, shootouts are no longer used to decide a winner. Instead, the games continue until a goal is scored—sudden death. But sometimes the end of the game isn't so sudden. Twice, games have gone into a sixth overtime before someone scores the deciding goal. That's almost the length of two more full games!

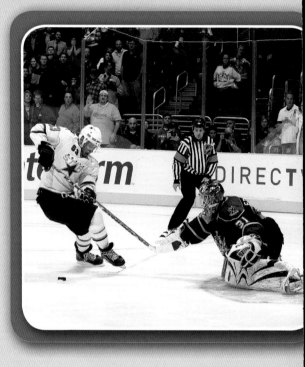

WORTH THE WAIT

The longest Stanley Cup-clinching game took place in 1999 when the Dallas Stars beat the Buffalo Sabres 2-1. Brett Hull beat goalie Dominik Hasek with the rebound goal, which came with 5 minutes, 9 seconds remaining in the third overtime.

Date	Score	Game Time	Winning Goal
March 24, 1936	Red Wings 1, Maroons 0	2:56:30	Mud Bruneteau
April 3, 1933	Maple Leafs 1, Bruins 0	2:44:46	Ken Doraty
May 4, 2000	Flyers 2, Penguins 1	2:32:01	Keith Primeau
April 24, 2003	Ducks 4, Stars 3	2:20:48	Petr Sykora
April 24, 1996	Penguins 3, Capitals 2	2:19:15	Petr Nedved
April 11, 2007	Canucks 5, Stars 4	2:18:06	Henrik Sedin
March 23, 1943	Maple Leafs 3, Red Wings 2	2:10:18	Jack McLean
May 4, 2008	Stars 2, Sharks 1	2:09:03	Brenden Morrow
March 28, 1930	Canadiens 2, Rangers 1	2:08:52	Gus Rivers
April 18, 1987	Islanders 3, Capitals 2	2:08:47	Pat LaFontaine

Note: A regular game has 1:00:00 of playing time

Joe Thornton fights for the puck during the May 4, 2008, matchup against the Stars.

GREATEST GOALS

Great plays are made all over the rink during a hockey game. There are incredible saves, pretty passes, and bone-crushing hits. But some of the greatest plays of all are the awe-inspiring goals.

HEXTALL SHOOTS ... AND SCORES?

Philadelphia Flyers goaltender Ron Hextall did a lot more than stop pucks. He was considered one of the best puck-handling and passing goalies in the league. On December 8, 1987, Hextall did something no other goaltender had ever done before— shoot and score a goal. It happened late in the game after the Bruins had pulled their goalie for an extra skater. Hextall stopped the puck and fired it the length of the ice. It was a bull's-eye, right into the empty net. Only eight other goaltenders have scored a goal in NHL history.

ORR TAKES FLIGHT

Bobby Orr was a defenseman who wasn't afraid to leave the blue line and get in front of the net. It's what made him one of the greatest players of all time. During the 1970 Stanley Cup Finals, Orr won the championship for the Boston Bruins with one of the greatest overtime goals. Orr passed to teammate Derek Sanderson, who was behind the St. Louis Blues' net. Orr then skated down the goal line toward the net. He got the puck back from Sanderson and tapped it into the net before being tripped and flying through the air in celebration.

FACT:

In 1979 the New York Islanders' Billy Smith became the first goalie to be credited with a goal. The score happened after the puck bounced off his chest pad and was accidentally shot in the other net by an opposing player. Smith got the credit because he was the last person on his team to touch the puck before it went into the net.

"THE GOAL"

Alex Ovechkin wasn't in the league long before he had a highlight reel that would make veteran players jealous. During his rookie season, he scored what Washington Capitals fans simply refer to as "the goal." After racing down the ice on a rush, Ovechkin appeared to be checked to the ice. He fell to the ice with his back to the goal and his hands above his head. Somehow the future superstar still found a way to shoot the puck past the goalie and into the net.

A LEGG UP

Great goals aren't just scored in the NHL. College players have made jaws drop too. In 1996 University of Michigan forward Mike Legg was alone with the puck behind the University of Minnesota net. He picked up the puck with his stick and tucked it into the upper corner of the goal. It looked more like a lacrosse goal than a hockey goal. The Wolverines went on to beat the Gophers in the NCAA tournament game.

WHICH WAY DID HE GO?

In 2008 Columbus Blue Jackets star forward Rick Nash secured a spot on the list of all-time great goals. He carried the puck into the attacking zone where two defensemen were preparing to stop him. He faked out one defenseman, then another, and then faked out the Coyotes' goaltender before scoring. The goal has been watched on YouTube more than 1 million times.

THE RECORDS

Believe it or not, Wayne Gretzky doesn't own every NHL record— it just seems that way. "The Great One" retired as the all-time leader in goals, assists, and points. But who's behind him on the list? Who has the most power-play goals? Who holds the goaltending records? Gretzky's marks seem well out of reach. Do you think the others can be broken?

WAYNE GRETZKY

Career Goals

1.	Wayne Gretzky	894
2.	Gordie Howe	801
3.	Brett Hull	741
4.	Marcel Dionne	731
5.	Phil Esposito	717

Career Assists

1.	Wayne Gretzky	1,963
2.	Ron Francis	1,249
3.	Mark Messier	1,193
4.	Ray Bourque	1,169
5.	Paul Coffey	1,135

Career Points (goals + assists)

1.	Wayne Gretzky	2,857
2.	Mark Messier	1,887
3.	Gordie Howe	1,850
4.	Ron Francis	1,798
5.	Marcel Dionne	1,771

MARK MESSIER

Career Game-winning Goals

1. Phil Esposito — 118
2. Jaromir Jagr — 112
3. Brett Hull — 110
4. Brendan Shanahan — 109
5. Guy Lafleur — 97

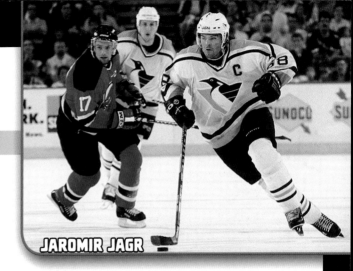

JAROMIR JAGR

Career Penalties in Minutes

1. Tiger Williams — 3,966
2. Dale Hunter — 3,565
3. Tie Domi — 3,515
4. Marty McSorley — 3,381
5. Bob Probert — 3,300

Career Goaltending Wins

1. Martin Brodeur* — 602
2. Patrick Roy — 551
3. Ed Belfour — 484
4. Curtis Joseph — 454
5. Terry Sawchuk — 447

Career Shutouts

1. Martin Brodeur* — 110
2. Terry Sawchuk — 103
3. George Hainsworth — 94
4. Glenn Hall — 84
5. Jacques Plante — 82

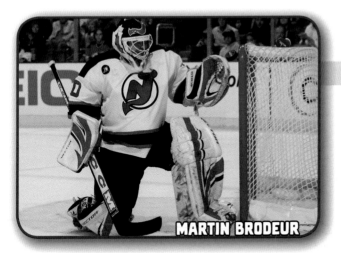

MARTIN BRODEUR

Career Goals-against Average

1. Alec Connell — 1.91
2. George Hainsworth — 1.93
3. Charlie Gardiner — 2.02
4. Lorne Chabot — 2.03
5. Tiny Thompson — 2.08

Career Save Percentage

1. Dominik Hasek — .922
2. Roberto Luongo* — .919
3. Tim Thomas* — .918
4. Henrik Lundqvist* — .918
5. Tomas Vokoun — .916

* still active

CHAPTER 5

FAN FAVORITES

ARENAS

OUT WITH THE OLD

The NHL's Original Six teams—the Canadiens, Maple Leafs, Bruins, Blackhawks, Red Wings, and Rangers—played in magnificent old buildings for most of their history. Those arenas included the Montreal Forum, Maple Leaf Gardens, Boston Garden, Chicago Stadium, the Detroit Olympia Stadium, and an older version of Madison Square Garden. The teams have since moved from those old "barns" and into state-of-the-art arenas. One of the oldest arenas in the NHL is Nassau Veterans Memorial Coliseum, home to the Islanders since 1972.

DETROIT RED WINGS' JOE LOUIS ARENA

MINNESOTA WILD'S XCEL ENERGY CENTER

IN WITH THE NEW

Many new arenas have been built for NHL teams in recent years. The newest building is the Penguins' Consol Energy Center, which the team moved into in 2010. Many surveys have named the Minnesota Wild's Xcel Energy Center as the best building in the league for both fans and players—of all ages. Besides being home to the self-proclaimed State of Hockey's professional team, it is also home to a college hockey championship and the boys and girls high school state championships.

SIT IN THE SADDLE

One of the most unique NHL arenas is the Flames' Pengrowth Saddledome. Why is it called the Saddledome? Because it looks like a giant could straddle the building and ride it across western Canada. Like a saddle atop a horse, the building has a low middle and high ends. The Saddledome was the site of Olympic hockey and figure skating in 1988, and the Flames played in three Stanley Cup Finals series there.

ON FROZEN POND

Each year the NHL honors hockey's outdoor beginnings by playing a New Year's Day game outside in the cold—and sometimes the snow. The NHL Winter Classic isn't played on lakes or rivers, though. A rink is set up in an outdoor stadium. The first was played in 2008 in Buffalo's Ralph Wilson Stadium. Then it went to a pair of historic baseball stadiums: Chicago's Wrigley Field in 2009 and Boston's Fenway Park in 2010.

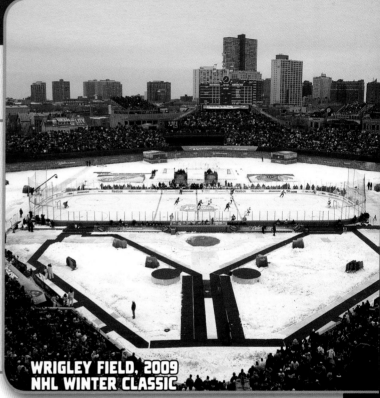

WRIGLEY FIELD, 2009
NHL WINTER CLASSIC

Five Largest Hockey Arenas

1. Bell Centre (Canadiens)	22,500
2. United Center (Blackhawks)	20,500
3. Joe Louis Arena (Red Wings)	20,066
4. Scotiabank Place (Senators)	20,004
5. St. Pete Times Forum (Lightning)	19,758

NHL TROPHIES

The NHL is known for its trophies, which it hands out to its best players every season. The Hart Trophy has been given out to the league MVP since 1924, and the Conn Smythe Trophy has gone to the best player in the playoffs since 1965.

STANLEY CUP

No trophy in hockey—perhaps in any sport—is as famous as the Stanley Cup. The Cup is awarded to the team that wins the NHL playoff championship every season. The oldest trophy in professional sports, the Cup was first donated to hockey in 1892 by Sir Frederick Arthur Stanley, known as Lord Stanley of Preston. When a team wins the Cup, each player's name is engraved on the silver trophy, and each player gets to take it home for one day in the offseason.

STANLEY CUP FACTS

- The Canadiens' Henri Richard had his name engraved on the Cup a record 11 times as a player.

- Jean Beliveau has his name on the Cup 17 times as both a player and coach.

- Scotty Bowman won the Cup a record nine times as a coach.

- The first team to engrave its roster on the Cup was the Montreal Wanderers in 1907.

- The Cup is 35 ¼ inches (90 cm) high and weighs 34 ½ pounds (15.6 kg). It continues to grow because sections are added to fit the names of the new champions.

NHL AWARD TROPHIES

Art Ross Trophy

leading point scorer

Bill Masterton Memorial Trophy

player who displays perseverance and dedication to hockey

Calder Memorial Trophy

rookie of the year

Conn Smythe Trophy

most valuable player of the playoffs

Cam Ward with the 2006 Conn Smythe Trophy

Frank J. Selke Trophy

top defensive forward

Hart Memorial Trophy

most valuable player

Jack Adams Award

coach of the year

James Norris Memorial Trophy

top defenseman

King Clancy Memorial Trophy

player who displays leadership on the ice and in the community

Lady Byng Memorial Trophy

player who displays gentlemanly conduct

Maurice "Rocket" Richard Trophy

leading goal scorer

Ted Lindsay Award

MVP as voted on by the players

Vezina Trophy

top goaltender

William M. Jennings Trophy

goaltender with the lowest goals-against average

GREAT NICKNAMES

From "Mr. Hockey" Gordie Howe and "The Great One" Wayne Gretzky to Sid "The Kid" Crosby, hockey players are known for their nicknames. Rarely do players get called by their birth names when they're on the rink. Some nicknames have stuck throughout NHL history.

SID "THE KID" CROSBY

"THE GOLDEN JET" BOBBY HULL

In an era before helmets, Bobby Hull was known for his fast skating and his flowing blond hair.

BERNIE "BOOM BOOM" GEOFFRION

The Canadiens star of the 1950s got his great nickname from the sound that is made by the shot he supposedly invented—the slap shot.

MAURICE "ROCKET" RICHARD

The Canadiens' star was known for his intensity and speed, skating like a rocket around the Montreal Forum. He went to the All-Star Game 13 times and entered the NHL Hall of Fame in 1961.

"MR. ZERO" FRANK BRIMSEK

As a goalie with the Bruins in 1939–1940, Frank Brimsek earned his nickname by recording 10 shutouts and a pair of amazing scoreless streaks. One streak lasted 231 minutes, 54 seconds, and another spanned 220 minutes, 24 seconds en route to a Stanley Cup. He had 40 shutouts in his 10-year career.

DAVE "THE HAMMER" SCHULTZ

One of the great fighters in NHL history, Dave Schultz was one of the Flyers' famed "Broad Street Bullies." He led the NHL in penalty minutes four times during his career.

TRIVIA

Can you match these 10 nicknames to the correct player?

1. The Wrecking Ball   Al Arbour

2. The Red Baron   Gordon Berenson

3. The Monster   Derek Boogard

4. The Russian Rocket   Adam Brown

5. The Flying Scotsman   Pavel Bure

6. Radar   Johan Franzen

7. The Finnish Flash   Jonas Gustavsson

8. Cyclone   Mark Recchi

9. The Boogie Man   Teemu Selanne

10. The Mule   Marvin Wentworth

Answer: 1. Mark Recchi 2. Gordon Berenson 3. Jonas Gustavsson 4. Pavel Bure 5. Adam Brown 6. Al Arbour 7. Teemu Selanne 8. Marvin Wentworth 9. Derek Boogaard 10. Johan Franzen

53

OLYMPIC HOCKEY

The NHL isn't the only place to showcase the great game of hockey. Some of the most exciting moments on the ice have taken place during the Winter Olympics.

The United States men's hockey team has won two gold medals, one in 1960 and one in 1980. In 1980 the young U.S. team pulled off the "Miracle on Ice." Behind the heroics of captain Mike Eruzione and goalie Jim Craig, the U.S. upset the favored Soviet Union 4-3. Eruzione scored the game-winning goal, and Craig made 39 saves. Two days later the Americans defeated Finland 4-2 for the gold medal.

USA'S 1980 OLYMPIC HOCKEY TEAM

In 2010 in Vancouver, British Columbia, Canada, the United States men played in one of the most memorable Olympic hockey games. In the early rounds of the Olympic tournament, the Americans upset the Canadians 5-3. In a final-game rematch Canada took an early lead and held it for most of the game. The game headed to overtime after U.S. forward Zach Parise tied the game with 25 seconds left in regulation. Penguins star Sidney Crosby gave the Canadians the gold medal with a thrilling goal in sudden-death overtime.

CANADA'S 2010 MEN'S OLYMPIC HOCKEY TEAM

WOMEN'S HOCKEY

Women and girls play at many levels: youth, high school, college, and international play. The NHL has expressed interest in creating a professional hockey league for women as well. Women's hockey has been an Olympic sport since 1998, when the United States won the gold medal in Nagano, Japan. Canada has won the last three gold medals, with the U.S. taking silver in 2002 and 2010. In Vancouver, Marie Philip Poulin scored two goals, and Shannon Szabados made 28 saves in Canada's 2-0 win over the Americans.

Women's Canadian gold medal hockey team, 2010

COLLEGE HOCKEY

A popular level of hockey in the United States is the college game. The game is played mostly in the West, Midwest, and the Northeast. Some NHL stars who have won the Hobey Baker Award as college hockey's best player include Neal Broten (Minnesota, 1981), Paul Kariya (Maine, 1993), Chris Drury (Boston University, 1998), and Ryan Miller (Michigan State, 2001).

Boston College versus University of Wisconsin, 2010 NCAA Men's National Championship

RECENT NCAA DIVISION 1 WINNERS

Men's		Women's	
2010	Boston College Eagles	2010	Minnesota Duluth Bulldogs
2009	Boston University Terriers	2009	Wisconsin Badgers
2008	Boston College Eagles	2008	Minnesota Duluth Bulldogs
2007	Michigan State Spartans	2007	Wisconsin Badgers
2006	Wisconsin Badgers	2006	Wisconsin Badgers

AROUND THE NHL

MASKED MEN

Goalies are some of the game's most interesting characters. One place where they show off their personality is on their protective masks. Many of the masks have detailed pictures painted on the helmets. The Buffalo Sabres' Ryan Miller's helmet features the head of a red-eyed, blue-and-yellow buffalo. Former New York Rangers goalie Mike Richter had the head of the Statue of Liberty on his mask. Two fearsome skeletons creep along the helmet of Evgeni Nabokov of the San Jose Sharks.

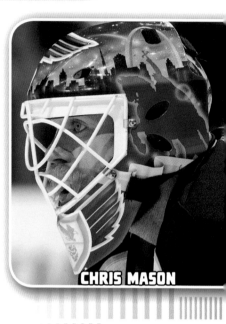
CHRIS MASON

EVGENI NABOKOV

BREAKING BARRIERS

On January 18, 1958, history was made when Bruins winger Willie O'Ree took the ice. O'Ree was the first black player to participate in an NHL game. The Canada native had a short professional career. He played in just two games that season and 43 games in 1960–1961 when he scored four goals. In 1992 the Lightning made history when they signed goaltender Manon Rheaume to a contract. She was the first and only woman to play in the NHL. Her only NHL playing time came during an exhibition game, but she also had a short minor-league career.

A REAL DREAM TEAM

In 1987 Canada put together one of the finest hockey teams ever assembled to compete for the Canada Cup. Long before NHL players were allowed to skate in the Olympics, the Canada Cup was an international tournament featuring pro players. Imagine a team with Mario Lemieux passing to Wayne Gretzky and back to Lemieux for a goal. Canada also had Mark Messier at forward, Paul Coffey on defense, and Grant Fuhr in front of the net. "For me," Gretzky said, "it was probably the best hockey I've ever played."

ROLLER HOCKEY

You don't need ice to play hockey. It can be played on wheels too. Some people play roller hockey outdoors in the summer. Others play indoors on specially made roller-skating surfaces. There is even a professional inline-skate league called Major League Roller Hockey. The league has teams in Chicago, Detroit, Washington, and other cities. Nashville Predators forward Joel Ward played roller hockey before working his way to the NHL.

MASCOTS

Hockey mascots add even more entertainment to an already exciting sport. They liven up the crowd with loud, energetic cheers. They provide comic relief by humorously falling over or pulling pranks on the refs or members of the other team. Some mascots, such as Al the Octopus, were created by traditions. These playful creatures are sometimes known as the faces of the franchises, and they are definitely parts of their teams.

FACT:

Four NHL teams have never had a mascot: the Dallas Stars, Edmonton Oilers, New York Rangers, and Philadelphia Flyers.

S.J. SHARKIE OF THE SAN JOSE SHARKS

HARVEY THE HOUND

The first mascot to patrol the stands of an NHL game was the Calgary Flames' dog, Harvey the Hound. Harvey is 6 feet 6 inches (198 cm), weighs 200 pounds (91 kg), and has a long, red tongue hanging from his open mouth. Although mascots usually don't talk, Harvey's tongue has gotten him into some trouble. During a game against the Edmonton Oilers, he started taunting the opposing players from behind the glass. Frustrated Oilers coach Craig MacTavish reached up and ripped the tongue out of the dog's mouth, tossing it into the crowd.

ICEBURGH

Pittsburgh's mascot, a giant Penguin named Iceburgh, is known for making fans smile both during games and outside the arena. The beloved penguin is also a movie star. In 1995 he appeared in the action movie *Sudden Death* with Jean Claude Van Damme.

NORDY

When the Minnesota Wild unveiled its logo in 2000, no one knew what it was. A bear? A cougar? A wolf? Seven years later, the Wild's mascot, Nordy, skated onto the ice for the first time. But the costume didn't clear anything up. All you can say is that he is a wild animal from the north woods with a green "M" on his forehead. He also has a golden mullet—otherwise known as hockey hair—flowing off the back of his neck.

AL THE OCTOPUS

One of the slimiest hockey playoff traditions started in 1952. That's when an octopus was first thrown onto the ice during a Red Wings home playoff game in Detroit. The creature's eight legs represented the eight post-season wins a team needed to capture the Stanley Cup. Although more games are now needed to win the Cup, the tradition continues, and fans still find ways to toss octopuses on the ice. The sea creature is now the Red Wings' unofficial mascot. A giant, inflated purple octopus named Al hangs from the rafters of Joe Louis Arena.

TIMELINE

1873	The rules of hockey are first written by James Creighton in Montreal
1877	The first organized hockey team is formed at McGill University in Montreal
1891	The first women's hockey games are played
1893	The first Stanley Cup games are played
1909	The Montreal Canadiens are founded
1917	The National Hockey League is formed; the Seattle Metropolitans of the Pacific Coast Hockey Association become the first American team to win the Stanley Cup
1920	Men's hockey is played in the Olympics for the first time; Canada takes the gold medal in Antwerp, Belgium
1924	The Boston Bruins play in the first NHL game in the United States
1942	The Brooklyn Americans (formerly the New York Americans) fold, leaving the NHL with its Original Six teams
1948	The University of Michigan wins the first NCAA men's hockey championship
1967	The NHL expands to 12 teams
1972	The new professional league called the World Hockey Association is formed; several NHL stars, including Chicago's Bobby Hull, jump to the new league
1978	Wayne Gretzky makes his professional debut with the Indianapolis Racers of the WHA; eight games into the season he was traded to Edmonton
1979	The WHA's remaining teams—the Edmonton Oilers, Quebec Nordiques, Hartford Whalers, and the Winnipeg Jets—merge into the NHL

1980	The United States pulls off the "Miracle on Ice" during the Olympics, upsetting the mighty Soviet Union
1998	NHL players compete in the Olympics; women's hockey is played in the Olympics for the first time
1999	Wayne Gretzky retires as the NHL's all-time leading scorer
2000	The Minnesota Wild and the Columbus Blue Jackets are added to the NHL, bringing the total number of teams to 30
2004	The NHL season doesn't start because of a disagreement between team owners and players; the season is canceled and, for the first time since 1919, the Stanley Cup was not awarded
2005	Shootouts after overtimes are introduced to regular-season NHL games, meaning there are no more tie games
2010	Sidney Crosby scores the game-winning goal in overtime as Canada defeats the United States 3-2 in the men's gold medal game of the Winter Olympics in Vancouver

TRIVIA

Match the current NHL team with its original home.

Carolina Hurricanes	Inglewood, California
Dallas Stars	Landover, Maryland
Phoenix Coyotes	Quebec City, Quebec, Canada
Washington Capitals	San Francisco, California
Calgary Flames	Atlanta, Georgia
New Jersey Devils	Winnipeg, Manitoba, Canada
Colorado Avalanche	Boston, Massachusetts
San Jose Sharks	Bloomington, Minnesota
Los Angeles Kings	Kansas City, Missouri

Answer: Hurricanes—Boston; Stars—Bloomington; Coyotes—Winnipeg; Capitals—Landover; Flames—Atlanta; Devils—Kansas City; Avalanche—Quebec City; Sharks—San Francisco; Kings—Inglewood

GLOSSARY

BLUE LINE: one of two blue-colored lines on the rink that mark the outside of the offensive zone; for the attacking team, offsides is called if the players cross the blue line before the puck

BREAKAWAY: play in which a skater with the puck ends up alone against the goaltender

CENTER: forward who plays in the middle of the rink

COMPOSITE: made up of different parts or materials

DEFENSEMAN: one of two players who stays by the ice's blue line to help defend his goal

DEFICIT: the number of goals a team is losing by

DEKE: fancy move with the stick or the body to fake out a defender or goalie

DYNASTY: period of years in which one team dominates play and wins multiple championships

EXPANSION: the growth of the NHL by adding new teams

GOALTENDER: player who plays in front of the net and tries to stop the other team from scoring

LEFT WING: forward who plays on the left side of the rink

POINTS: total scoring; goals plus assists

POWER PLAY: period of time when a team has an advantage because the other team is short-handed with one or more players in the penalty box

REGULATION: time designated for a full game, not including overtime; regulation is 60 minutes in the NHL

RIGHT WING: forward who plays on the right side of the rink

WRISTERS: wrist shots

READ MORE

Doeden, Matt. *The Greatest Hockey Records*. Mankato, Minn.: Capstone Press, 2009.

Latimer, Clay. *VIP Pass to a Pro Hockey Game: From the Locker Room to the Press Box*. Mankato, Minn.: Capstone Press, 2011.

Sandler, Michael. *Hockey: Miracle On Ice*. New York: Bearport Publishing, 2006.

Shea, Therese. *Hockey Stars*. New York: Children's Press, 2007.

Thomas, Keltie. *Inside Hockey! The Legends, Facts and Feats That Made the Game*. Toronto: Maple Tree Press, 2008.

INTERNET SITES

FactHound offers a safe, fun way to find Internet sites related to this book. All of the sites on FactHound have been researched by our staff.

Here's all you do:

Visit www.facthound.com

Type in this code: 9781429654692

Super-cool stuff!

Check out projects, games and lots more at
www.capstonekids.com

INDEX